THE BATTLE OF LEPANTO

The Brutal Defeat of the Ottoman Empire

Written by Gauthier Godart
In collaboration with Romain Parmentier
Translated by Carly Probert

History **50MINUTES**.com

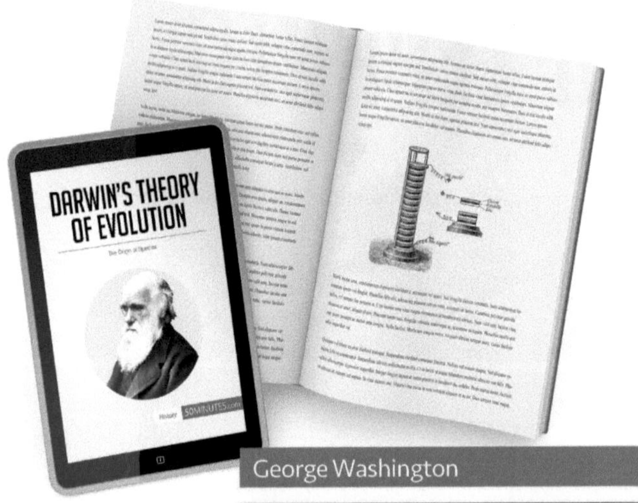

THE BATTLE OF LEPANTO

KEY INFORMATION

- **When:** 7 October 1571
- **Where:** Gulf of Patras, near Lepanto (known as Naupaktos in Greece today)
- **Context:** The conflict between the Christian West and the Ottoman Empire throughout the 16th century
- **Belligerents:** The Holy League consisting of Spain (and its Italian possessions, namely Naples and Sicily), the Republic of Venice and the Papal States, against the Ottoman Empire
- **Commanders and leaders:**
  - Don Juan of Austria, the Grand Admiral in charge of the supreme command of the Western fleet (1545-1578)
  - Uluj Ali, admiral in charge of the left wing of the Ottoman fleet (1520-1587)
- **Outcome:** Victory of the Holy League
- **Victims:**
  - Western camp: approximately 7 500 dead and 20 000 wounded
  - Ottoman camp: approximately 30 000 dead or wounded, and 3 500 prisoners

INTRODUCTION

On 7 October 1571, off the port of Lepanto, two gigantic fleets came face to face. On the one side were the ships of the Holy League, a recent and relatively fragile alliance of the Papal States, Spain and the Republic of Venice; on the other side, the immense and formidable Ottoman fleet.

This meeting was one of the consequences of the rise of violence against Christians. Angered by the repeated attacks of the Ottoman fleet and especially by the seizing of the island of Cyprus a year earlier which belonged to the Republic of Venice, they decided to attack the Ottoman Empire. However, the Christians were not very confident, and rightly so: the men they faced were seasoned fighters who had long demonstrated their effectiveness at sea.

At noon, when the Christians rose the banner of the Holy League on the orders of the great admiral Don Juan of Austria and the Muslim side fell to their knees in prayer, tensions became palpable. Aware of their overwhelming numerical superiority and made confident by their many successes in fighting at sea, Admiral Ali Pasha (died in 1571) and his men rejoiced in anticipation of their victory.

Yet, the naval battle, which would remain one of the largest in history, concluded in a way that defied all odds: after a few hours of heavy fighting, the Ottomans, to their great surprise, were thrown off balance. Their fleet was destroyed, and the Christians, in a mixture of surprise and relief, celebrated their victory.

POLITICAL AND SOCIAL CONTEXT

THE FIGHT FOR CONTROL OF THE MEDITERRANEAN

Since the day they seized Constantinople from the Byzantines in 1453, thereby causing the fall of the Eastern Roman Empire, the Turks focused all their efforts on expanding their territory in Eastern Europe, as well as in the Mediterranean basin. Not content with controlling most of the African coast and standing a good chance of becoming the masters of the Eastern side, they moved more and more regularly towards the Western Mediterranean.

From the early 16th century, the Turks multiplied raids on the Italian and Spanish coasts, to the great displeasure of the Kingdom of Spain. After looting the coastal towns and villages, they left laden with new riches and humans destined for slavery or ransom. Many countries felt threatened by this empire that continued to gain ground.

Spain, which had long suffered from attacks, made a first attempt to slow the advance of the Ottoman Empire, sometime after the abdication of the German Emperor Charles V (1500-1558). It was then decided that the territory, the Italian possessions and the Netherlands would be inherited by his son, Phillip II (1527-1598), while the imperial title would be returned, two years later, to the brother of Charles V, Ferdinand I of Habsburg (Archduke of Austria, King of Hungary and Bohemia, 1503-1564). Anxious to follow in the footsteps of his father, Philip II quickly became the new representative of Catholicism. To prove himself, he got involved on two fronts:

- In the north, in the Spanish Netherlands that were shaken by the Protestant Reformation;
- In the Mediterranean, which was constantly targeted by the Ottomans.

At the time, the gigantic Ottoman Empire was shaken by a serious crisis of succession. Suleiman I, known as "Suleiman the Magnificent" (1494-1566), a great conqueror considered to be one of the most prominent princes of the 16th century, had several potential heirs. As there was no legislation to establish an order of succession, the sultan's sons, unable to come to an agreement, quarreled over the possession of the empire.

Philip II, warned of this crisis, decided to take advantage of the relative weakening of the enemy to strike. Therefore, in 1559 he sent a fleet towards the island of Djerba, which was under his control and which, due to its position off the North African coast, was an excellent starting point to attack against the "Muslim enemy" and recover the city of Tripoli, which had fallen to the Ottomans. Nonetheless, this attack would never occur: on 12 May 1560, the fleet of Suleiman I attacked the Spaniards and destroyed them.

The humiliation was painful and stimulated a desire for revenge. Therefore, from 1561, shipyards multiplied on the Spanish and Italian coasts: henceforth, the aim was to build a fleet that would rival that of the Turks and bring them to an end.

THE CAPTURE OF CYPRUS: THE TRIGGER OF THE BATTLE

On 8 September 1566, the great Suleiman died and his son, Selim II, known as "Selim the Sot" (1524-1574), who managed to oust his brothers, succeeded him as head of the Ottoman Empire. The new sovereign did not possess his father's greatness and seemed to avoid confrontation, which could have signaled some relief: he also concluded a peace treaty with Austria in 1568. However, although Selim was not as strong as his father, he nonetheless wished to establish himself as his worthy successor. With this in mind, he strengthened his fleet and secretly developed the operation to attack Cyprus.

Occupied by the Venetian Republic, Cyprus constituted not only an important commercial relay, but also one of the last major Western strangleholds in the eastern Mediterranean. The Ottomans thus landed there forcefully on 1 July 1570 and seized the capital, Nicosia, in no time. Once the island was conquered (with the exception of the port of Famagusta, which only fell after more than a year of resistance), the invaders decided to move westward and successively sailed to Crete and the Adriatic coast, also controlled by Venice.

GOOD TO KNOW

Equally proud and powerful, the Republic of Venice had been fiercely defending its independence for half a millennium when the Ottomans attacked Cyprus.

First dominated by the Byzantine Empire, it managed to break free from the 9th century onwards, but did not separate completely from its former master. On the contrary, it regularly help to defend it from various aggressors (Arab invasions, Normans, etc.). In doing so, it received many privileges, one of which was the permission to establish trading posts on the empire's coasts, giving it a prominent place in trade between the East and West.

In the centuries that followed, it was constantly expanding its power to eventually form a true maritime empire. Thus, at the time of the Battle of Lepanto, it still controlled many trading posts along the coast of the Adriatic Sea and the Mediterranean Sea, and part of the north-east of Italy.

POPE PIUS V AND THE HOLY LEAGUE

Faced with the invasion of Cyprus which was perceived as a new provocation, Western reaction was immediate and found its initiator in Pope Pius V (1504-1572). Wishing to help the Venetians and particularly to motivate a crusade against the Ottoman Empire, from 1570 he displayed a vast diplomatic agenda, mainly oriented towards Spain and the Republic of Venice.

However, his task was very arduous. In Spain, Philip II showed little concern with the rescue of Venice, which he considered too close to the Muslim infidels with whom it did business. But, he still remembered the defeat of 1560 and the idea of a large-scale attack against the Ottoman Empire seemed quite attractive to him. Therefore, he eventually gave in to the insistence of the Pope.

Hesitation came mostly from the Venetians themselves. Drawing all their power from their control of trade between East and West, they showed little inclination to oppose the Ottomans, even though they had seized their Cypriot territory.

It was not until 25 May 1571 (almost one year later) that they finally formed an alliance under the name of the Holy League. Through this, Spain, the Republic of Venice and the Papal States agreed to each provide 200 galleys to fight the Ottoman Empire. The supreme command of the fleet created was entrusted to the half-brother of Philip II, Don Juan of Austria.

COMMANDERS AND LEADERS

DON JUAN OF AUSTRIA, SPANISH GRAND ADMIRAL

Born in 1545 from the illegitimate union of Charles V and Barbara Blomberg (1527-1597), Don Juan of Austria, a Spanish prince whose first name was originally Jeromín, was brought up away from the court, in strict secrecy.

It was not until the age of 11 that he first met his father, who had just abdicated in favor of his legitimate son, Philip II. Thereby respecting the will of Charles V, the latter received Jeromín into the Spanish court, giving him a welcome worthy of a blood brother, and a new name: Don Juan of Austria.

Destined for a religious career, the young man refused it and repeatedly expressed a desire to prove himself in the military. His half-brother gave him the opportunity to do so, and in 1568, appointed him to go to the Mediterranean and fight the Barbary pirates (from the land situated to the northwest of Africa), allies of the Ottomans.

Having accomplished his mission successfully, he was responsible for quelling the revolt of the Moriscos the following year, which had gone on since 1568. These Muslims who had stayed in Spain after the Reconquista and had been officially and often forcibly converted to Catholicism, were protesting violently against the various measures taken against them, first by Charles V, then by Philip II (mass expulsion, ban against showing religious affiliation, etc.). Don

Juan put an end to it in 1570 and, thanks to the success and popularity he derived from this action, he was then called upon to command the fleet of the Holy League, a role he fully assumed and which constituted the peak of his military career.

At Lepanto on 7 October 1571, he proved himself to be a great leader of men: he spent more than an hour motivating his soldiers before engaging in combat. He also sought to maintain a climate of fervor among them and to remind them that they were there by the will of God, and for the most honorable cause of all: Christianity. During the fight, he did not hesitate to put his own life on the line. He was seen storming the admiral flagship of the enemy fleet and, after a hard fight, he captured it. The great Ottoman Admiral Ali Pasha was defeated and, according to legend, Don Juan displayed his head on the top of the mast of the *Reale* (the admiral galley of the Holy League), thereby causing terror among the Ottomans and the jubilation of the Christians. After a few hours of an exceptionally violent fight, the Spanish prince emerged victorious.

Not content with this, Don Juan wanted to continue his exploits by attempting the re-conquest of Constantinople and Jerusalem, but Philip refused. The latter was more concerned with the Protestant rebellion that shook the north and decided to name his half-brother governor of the Netherlands, with orders to put an end to it. This was to be his last fight: he died of typhus in Namur (Belgium) on 1 October 1578.

ULUJ (OR ULUÇ) ALI, OTTOMAN ADMIRAL

Uluj Ali was born in Calabria in 1520, under the name of Giovanni Dionigi Galeni. A young man of lowly birth, he was kidnapped at the age of sixteen by one of the captains of the famous Barbary corsair Barbarossa.

First a slave on the galley of his captor, he converted to Islam, quickly managed to climb up the hierarchy and, after a few years, armed his first gun frigate to become a pirate himself. A fine sailor, it only took a few years for him to be considered one of the most daring corsairs of the Mediterranean.

Governor of Tripoli in 1565, he became the General Governor of Algiers three years later and was appointed to lead the left wing of the Ottoman fleet at Lepanto in 1571. During the battle, he tried to escape to attack the enemy fleet from behind, but the Genoese Admiral Giovanni Andrea Doria (1539-1606) he was facing had the same idea and hindered his movement. However, the Muslim privateer surprised everyone by ordering his squadron to turn around to step into the breach opened by the movement of Giovanni Andrea Doria. He managed to intercept several isolated ships, but Christian reinforcements soon arrived. Feeling his chances of victory slipping away, the pirate fled with what was left of his fleet, somehow becoming the only Ottoman to emerge victorious from Lepanto.

From 24 October, Sultan Selim II was warned of the disaster. Aware that, without the bravery and experience of Uluj Ali, the situation would have been worse, he decided to name him the Great Admiral of the Ottoman Fleet. Therefore, the former privateer emerged from the battle with full honors. He died on 21 June 1587.

ANALYSIS OF THE BATTLE

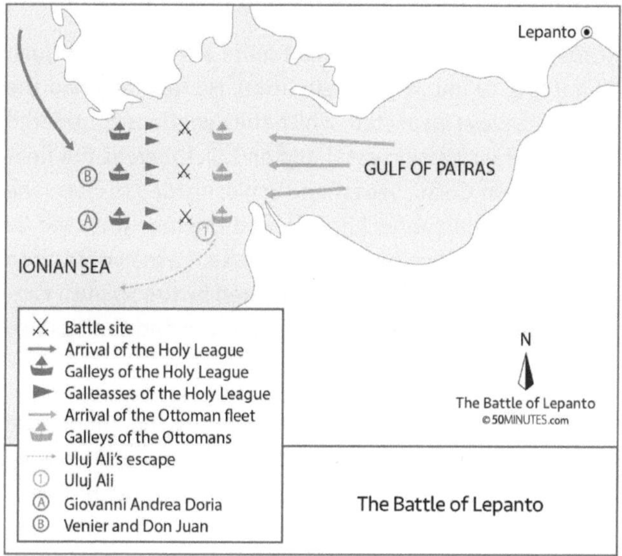

The Battle of Lepanto

BEFORE THE BATTLE: CHRISTIAN TENSIONS...

On 24 August 1571, the fleet of the Holy League gathered in Messina (East Sicily). Holding the meeting was not an easy task: the Spaniards felt nothing but contempt towards the Venetians and the Venetians felt the same. On one side, the young prince Don Juan, as supreme commander of the fleet, intended to establish his authority; on the other side, the Venetian Admiral Sebastiano Venier (1496-1578) could barely stand the duty to obey such an inexperienced young man. The situation did not improve when Don Juan, doubting the sailing and fighting abilities of the Venetians, forced Venier to welcome a contingent of Spaniards onto his ship.

Although Sebastiano Venier had quite a temper, Don Juan did nothing to improve the situation. He regularly had the Venetian galleys inspected, which the Venetians considered insulting. The situation escalated on 2 October: as the fleet anchored near Corfu, Sebastiano Venier needed to intervene in one of his galleys, as his crew and the men imposed by Don Juan were killing one another. He sent a man of trust to clarify the situation, but he was injured by the Spanish captain. Sebastiano Venier reacted firmly and had the Spanish captain hanged.

When he found out, Don Juan was furious and announced his desire to hang the Venetian Admiral in turn for making such a decision without his consent. Although things finally calmed down, the divide between the Venetians and Spaniards was clearly present.

...AND MUSLIM DEFECTIONS

On their side, the Muslims experienced some other problems. Their fleet was in campaign since the capture of Cyprus, which was over a year ago. The men were exhausted, sick, some were injured, and their morale was low.

It was under these conditions that they heard the news of the gathering of the enemy fleet in Messina. Aware that they could not resist them without taking a little rest and refueling, the Ottomans decided to withdraw to the port of

Lepanto. Uluj Ali was then tasked with debarking hundreds of sick and injured crew members in a safe place. But these defections were accompanied by numerous desertions: the men and their captains, thinking the expedition was complete and not believing in an attack from the Holy League, decided to return home. The Ottoman fleet was therefore weakened when it faced the Christians.

Despite this, when he learned that the Christian fleet was sailing to Lepanto, Admiral Ali Pasha refused to listen to those who advised him to stay under the cover of the walls and artillery of Lepanto and decided to go and meet the enemy.

Portrait of Ali Pasha, c. 1571.

A SURPRISING MEETING

When the two fleets came face to face at the end of the Gulf of Patras (Greece) in the morning of 7 October 1571, it came as a surprise to both sides. The Christians thought they would find the Ottomans barricaded in the port of Lepanto and the Ottomans expected their opponents to be much further away.

In total, 170 000 men faced one another, half of which were made up of rowers chosen from the slaves or prisoners. They were distributed more or less equally between the two fleets. Historians do not agree on the number of these ships, but the following figures can be put forward:

- the Holy League's fleet contained approximately 200 galleys, 6 galleasses and 30 naves;
- the Ottoman fleet contained approximately 230 galleys and 70 galiotes and frigates.

GOOD TO KNOW

- Galleys were ships with sails and oars. They could have one or two masts, but were primarily pro-pelled using paddles whose length varied between 11 and 15 meters. Aside from the command galleys, they were not equipped with artillery.
- Galiotes were small galleys.
- Frigates were small, fast warships. They had a sail and twenty rowers. Without artillery, they served as a support to the galleys.
- Galleasses were true floating artillery batteries. Originally created by the Venetians for the transit of precious goods between the East and the West, six of them were transformed into military ships by the Venetians soon after the creation of the

Holy League. They were armed with thirty guns placed along the sides and hundreds of harque-buses (gun invented in the early 16th century, measuring between 80 and 130 centimeters, with a range of about 50 meters).
- The naves were freighters used by the fleet of the Holy League.

The quantitative advantage therefore lay with the Ottomans, who had nearly 300 warships, against just over 200 on the Christian side. But the galleys of the Holy League were better equipped with artillery, and with their six galleasses, the Christians opposed the Ottomans with extraordinary firing power. This advantage was strengthened by the fact that they were much better equipped with harquebuses, which were far more deadly that the Turks bows for archery. Moreover, the Turks misjudged the Christian forces. Indeed, the information from their spies indicated that the enemy only had 150 galleys and gave no mention of galleasses. Therefore, they contemplated the fight ahead with confidence, even showing themselves to be mocking and provocative.

But their confidence soon vanished when the Christians got in combat order:

- At the center was Don Juan, with 62 galleys. In this position, he managed to close the Gulf of Patras, thus preventing the Ottomans from escaping towards the sea.
- In the north, the left wing was protected by 53 galleys.
- In the south, the right wing, led by Giovanni Andrea

Doria, was protected by 50 galleys.

The six galleasses, positioned forward, were divided equally among each of the fronts, and the remaining thirty galleys formed the rear. The Ottomans then responded by sending 56 ships towards the Christian left wing, 96 towards Don Juan and 94 to face Giovanni Andrea Doria. The remaining sixty ships stayed at the back.

Once the two fleets were in place, the great Ottoman Admiral Ali Pasha fired a salvo of artillery, signaling to Don Juan that he wanted a single combat. He responded: the battle began.

IN THE NORTH: THE OPENING OF HOSTILITIES

It was in the north that the Ottomans measured themselves up to the Venetian galleasses for the first time. The Turkish right wing advanced quickly on the Christian left wing, but this movement was violently interrupted by the fire of the two floating batteries. For a brief moment, the Turks were petrified: they did not expect such firepower, against which they seemed powerless. However, they quickly reorganized themselves and tried, more or less successfully, to override the two killing machines. Many of their galleys sank to the bottom of the sea, but the majority of their ships managed to perform the maneuver. They then separated into two groups: while one part of the fleet attempted to take the Christians from their side, along the sandbanks of the shore, the other continued to advance on them from the front.

Illustration depicting the Battle of Lepanto.

For a moment, the left wing of the Holy League was therefore in a dangerous situation. Caught between two fronts, it could barely withstand the onslaught and found it difficult to deal with the shower of arrows that struck it, particularly since the galleasses were no longer of much help. Overwhelmed by the Turkish fleet, the galleasses needed to turn around to rescue their own, which was a difficult maneuver for these heavy ships. However, the Christians succeeded, against all odds, in pushing back the ships that tried to attack them from behind. The Ottomans then had no choice but to take to the land and flee. Those who did not manage to get away were cut to pieces.

Now all that remained was the ships that retained their position and faced the Christians. Having seen the debacle, they became even more aggressive. But one of the Christian galleasses operated a turning maneuver, and another soon followed suit. The Ottomans were thus caught between the bulk of the left wing and the two galleasses. At the cost of heavy losses, the Christians finally brought them to an end.

IN THE CENTER: THE MEETING OF THE CHAMPIONS

Meanwhile, fighting also affected the center. The galleasses had come into action and wreaked havoc both in the enemy fleet and in the north. Several Ottoman galleys sank from the first bursts, others were forced to disrupt their formation to get away from the batteries. However, the ships that managed to survive gathered and faced the Christian center, which was inferior in number.

Here, the fighting was particularly fierce. The two fleets stormed suddenly, without bypassing attempts: in this case, it was a frontal collision.

At the heart of this horror was Don Juan's galley, that of the representative of Pope Pius V and that of Admiral Sebastiano Venier, the champions of Christianity. Ali Pasha tried to play on the element of surprise. Giving every reason to believe that he intended to storm the galley of Sebastiano Venier, at the last moment he nevertheless headed for that of Don Juan. The two galleys violently collided. The Spanish soldiers immediately began to fire their harquebuses, while the Venetians of Sebastiano Venier's galley stormed the stern (rear) of the Ottoman ship and boarded it. Ali Pasha died in the attack: his head was cut off by one of the assailants.

All around, the fighting continued to rage, but at the sight of the Holy League flag which had been hoisted on the ship of Ali Pasha, many Turks fled. The battle was not yet won for the Christians, who were still inferior in number compared to the enemy. After three hours of fighting, the Ottomans were defeated.

IN THE SOUTH: ULUJ ALI'S STRATEGY

While the fighting continued in the north and the center, in the south Uluj Ali began to get out of the Gulf to attack the Christian fleet from the rear. Seeing this, Giovanni Andrea Doria, commander of the right wing, took the same initiative and attempted to obstruct the Muslim privateer. However, the two galleasses that had been assigned to his fleet struggled to keep up with him. Not only was his fleet outnumbered by that of Uluj Ali, but a portion of it also misinterpreted his movement and remained behind, near the main body.

Taking advantage of the confusion, Uluj Ali suddenly rushed into the empty space left by the right wing and stormed the galleys that had remained behind, causing a real massacre. From there, he resumed the attack on the boats of Giovanni Andrea Doria, which resisted with difficulty, as the power was unbalanced.

Nonetheless, Christian reinforcements arrived: Don Juan's rear and galleys, which were done with the main part of the Ottoman forces, came to the rescue. Uluj Ali had no choice but to flee with thirty of his galleys. The Westerners pursued them, but did not manage to catch up.

THE OUTCOME OF THE BATTLE

At around 5:00pm, the fighting had almost come to an end. The victory was already attributed to the Christians and the Muslims who were still fighting only did so because they had no opening to escape. According to some accounts, the Ottomans, having exhausted their ammunition, had no choice but to launch their provisions on the enemy, causing nothing but laughter and disdain.

The celebration was short-lived, however. Among the debris, there were 12 Christian vessels. Although it had won the battle, the price was heavy for the Holy League: there were approximately 7 500 dead and nearly 20 000 wounded.

On the Muslim side, the collapse was complete. The Ottoman fleet was almost entirely destroyed, and the battle had cost them nearly 30 000 victims, dead or wounded, as well as the 3 500 prisoners. Furthermore, the Christians released around 15 000 of their slaves.

Defeat of the Ottomans.

Thus, despite the numerical advantage of the Ottomans, the Christian victory was total. Only a few Ottoman ships, guided by Uluj Ali, managed to escape the battle. Several factors allowed for this victory:

- Firstly, the Grand Admiral of the Ottoman fleet was

inexperienced. A soldier of the land force, he made his debut on the sea with the conquest of Cyprus. This lack of experience may explain why, on 7 October 1571, he decided to go to meet the enemy, instead of staying under the cover of the fortified walls and the artillery of the port of Lepanto;

- Secondly, the crew of the Ottoman fleet was very weak. Sailing on the Mediterranean for more than a year, they had not been given the opportunity to rest. This resulted in sickness, accidents, and a loss of motivation that led to the desertion of many men;

- Another factor of the Ottomans' weakness was the overwhelming superiority of the Christian fleet in terms of firepower. With their six galleasses and countless harquebuses held by their men, the Holy League largely made up for their numerical inferiority, ensuring their victory.

REPERCUSSIONS OF THE BATTLE

DIVISIONS WITHIN THE HOLY LEAGUE

After the battle, it is believed, in the West, that the Ottoman Empire came to an end. Indeed, the Ottoman Empire was deprived of its terrible fleet, had thousands of kilometers of coastline to defend, and had to face the uprising of many people who, on hearing the outcome of the Battle of Lepanto, violently rebelled. After more than a century of absolute dominance in the Mediterranean, the Turks seemed vulnerable for the first time. Therefore, this seemed like the ideal moment to deal them a fatal blow.

However, the conflicts undermining the Holy League had to be taken into account. Although the Spaniards and the Venetians managed to unite for a common cause for the duration of the battle, in the aftermath of the conflict, their rivalry resumed with even more vigor. The victors competed for prisoners and the spoils of war, and everyone wanted to take credit for the victory.

While all returned to dry land for the winter, the situation did not improve and a follow-up to the victory could not be agreed upon. Each had their own interests in mind, and Spain in particular did not want to move further into the eastern Mediterranean. This explains why, on 1 May 1572, the annual expedition of the Holy League against the Ottomans had not yet set sail. On this date, the Christians learned of the death of Pope Pius V. The Holy League was not to outlive him: all returned to their personal concerns and the common dream to end the Ottomans once and for all collapsed.

THE END OF OTTOMAN EXPANSIONISM

For their part, the Ottomans had already recovered. With all his energy and intelligence, the grand vizier (advisor) of Selim II, Mehmet Sokullu (1505-1579), quickly took matters into his own hands and ensured the reorganization of the empire. Command of the fleet was entrusted to Uluj Ali, the shipyards were improved and revolts were suppressed with bloodshed. Therefore, from 1572, the empire showed off its new fleet to the West, which was even more numerous and impressive than before the Battle of Lepanto.

Despite this renewed vigor, the Ottomans now seemed reluctant to provoke the West. Thus, the Battle of Lepanto brought an end to their expansionism and, in 1574, their re-conquest of Tunis (taken by Don Juan in 1573) marked the last significant conflict of the Ottoman fleet in the Mediterranean.

A year earlier, they even signed a peace treaty with the Venetians who, in exchange for the resumption of their trading activities, were forced to cede Cyprus. This disposition had serious consequences for the island. The Ottomans settled Anatolian peasants there, creating a Turkish Cypriot community that would set off a conflict with the Greek community on the island years later. The situation did not settle over time, since in 1974 Cyprus was split in two and today remains the last divided country in Europe.

Similarly, in 1578, the Spaniards established a truce with the Muslims: they could now focus on the Atlantic, after ensuring that their bases in the western Mediterranean were no longer threatened by the Ottomans.

Although historians have long considered the Battle of Lepanto to be the trigger of the progressive fall of the Ottoman Empire, above all it seems to have marked a shift in attitudes: the time of the Crusades was gone, and neither the East nor the West now aspired to a major confrontation, as their interests carried them in different directions. Spain was resolutely focused towards the Atlantic, Venice sought to restore its commercial business, and the Ottoman Empire was too busy with its internal affairs to continue its progress in the Mediterranean.

SUMMARY

- Since the capture of Constantinople by the Turks in 1453, the Ottoman Empire multiplied its attacks against Christians, never ceasing to loot towns and villages in order to extend its territory in Europe.
- Deciding to counter the Turks, Pope Pius V wanted to launch a crusade to curb their expansion. A year later, the Holy League was formed and its members undertook to provide ships each year to create a fleet to fight the

Ottomans.

- On the morning of 7 October 1571, the Christian and Ottoman fleets crossed paths in the Gulf of Patras. The Ottoman Grand Admiral Ali Pasha fired a salvo of artillery, to which Don Juan replied: the battle was underway.
- Hostilities were opened in the north where the Ottoman right wing faced the Venetian galleasses. The battleships opened fire, shocking the Ottomans with their firepower.
- By early afternoon, the galleys of Don Juan, the representative of Pope Pius V, and Sebastiano Venier faced those of Ali Pasha in the center. Ali Pasha was beheaded during the battle.
- Shortly after, in the south, Uluj Ali tried to leave the Gulf in order to attack the Christian fleet from the rear, putting Giovanni Andrea Doria in a difficult position. Seeing his intentions, the Holy League sent him reinforcements. Uluj Ali fled.
- Meanwhile, in the north, the Ottomans were caught between the left wing and the two Christian galleasses and were defeated by the Holy League.
- At around 5:00pm, the fighting had come to a gradual end: victory was granted to the Holy League.
- The battle ended with a disastrous record: on the Ottoman side, there were approximately 30 000 deaths and injuries, while the Christians' losses totaled approximately 7500.
- More than just a Christian victory, the Battle of Lepanto marked the end of the Crusades and the Ottoman expansionist ambitions.

FIND OUT MORE

BIBLIOGRAPHY

- Buresi, P. (No date) Lépante, Bataille de (1571). *Encyclopædia Universalis*. [Online]. [Accessed 5 December 2016]. Available from: <http://www.universalis.fr/encyclopedie/bataille-de-lepante/>
- Hélie, J. (2008) *Les relations internationales dans l'Europe moderne*. 1453-1789. Paris: Armand Collin.
- Lesure, M. (1972) *Lépante. La crise de l'Empire ottoman*. Paris: Gallimard.
- Mantran, R. (1989) *Histoire de l'Empire ottoman*. Paris: Fayard.
- Martinez Montávez, P. and Ruíz Bravo-Villasante, C. (1991) *L'Islam en Europe. L'essor, le déclin et l'héritage d'une civilisation*. Brussels: La Renaissance du Livre.
- Pérez, J. (1998) *L'Espagne du* xviie *siècle*. Paris: Armand Colin.

ADDITIONAL SOURCES

- Capponi, N. (2006) *Victory of the West: The Story of the Battle of Lepanto*. London: Macmillan.
- Crouzet-Pavan, E. (2005) *Venice Triumphant: The Horizons of a Myth*. Trans. Cochrane, L.G. Baltimore: John Hopkins University Press.
- Inalcik, H. (2000) *The Ottoman Empire: 1300-1600*. London: Phoenix Press.
- Kinross, J.P. (1979) *The Ottoman Centuries: The Rise and Fall of the Turkish Empire*. New York: William Morrow

and Company, Inc.
- Lane, F.C. (2013) *Venetian Ships and Shipbuilders of the Renaissance*. Baltimore: John Hopkins University Press.

ICONOGRAPHIC SOURCES

- Portrait of Ali Pasha, c. 1571. Royalty-free reproduction image.
- Illustration depicting the Battle of Lepanto. Royalty-free reproduction image.
- Defeat of the Ottomans. Royalty-free reproduction image.

DOCUMENTARIES

- *Lepanto 1571*. (1977) [Documentary]. Stefano Roncoroni. Dir. France.
- *The Battle of Lepanto*. (2004) [Documentary]. Marc Brasse. Dir. Germany.

IMPROVE YOUR GENERAL KNOWLEDGE

IN A BLINK OF AN EYE !

www.50minutes.com